A Bug's World

Hop with the Grasshoppers

By Karen Latchana Kenney
Illustrated by Lisa Hedicker

Content Consultant
Clyde Sorenson, PhD
Professor of Entomology
North Carolina State University

magic
wagon

visit us at www.abdopublishing.com

Published by Magic Wagon, a division of the ABDO Group, 8000 West 78th Street, Edina, Minnesota 55439.
Copyright © 2011 by Abdo Consulting Group, Inc. International copyrights reserved in all countries. All rights
reserved. No part of this book may be reproduced in any form without written permission from the publisher.

Looking Glass Library™ is a trademark and logo of Magic Wagon.

Printed in the United States of America, North Mankato, Minnesota.
042010
092010

Text by Karen Latchana Kenney
Illustrations by Lisa Hedicker
Edited by Amy Van Zee
Interior layout and design by Becky Daum
Cover design by Becky Daum

Library of Congress Cataloging-in-Publication Data
Kenney, Karen Latchana.
  Hop with the grasshoppers / by Karen Latchana Kenney ; Illustrated by Lisa Hedicker.
     p. cm. — (A bug's world)
  Includes bibliographical references and index.
  ISBN 978-1-60270-786-3
  1. Grasshoppers—Juvenile literature. I. Hedicker, Lisa, 1984- , ill. II. Title.
  QL508.A2K36 2011
  595.7'26—dc22
                        2009052914

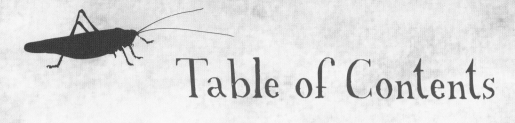

Table of Contents

Growing Grasshoppers

It is spring. Tiny, brown grasshopper eggs are hatching underground.

Out come nymphs. These baby grasshoppers look a lot like their parents, but they do not have wings.

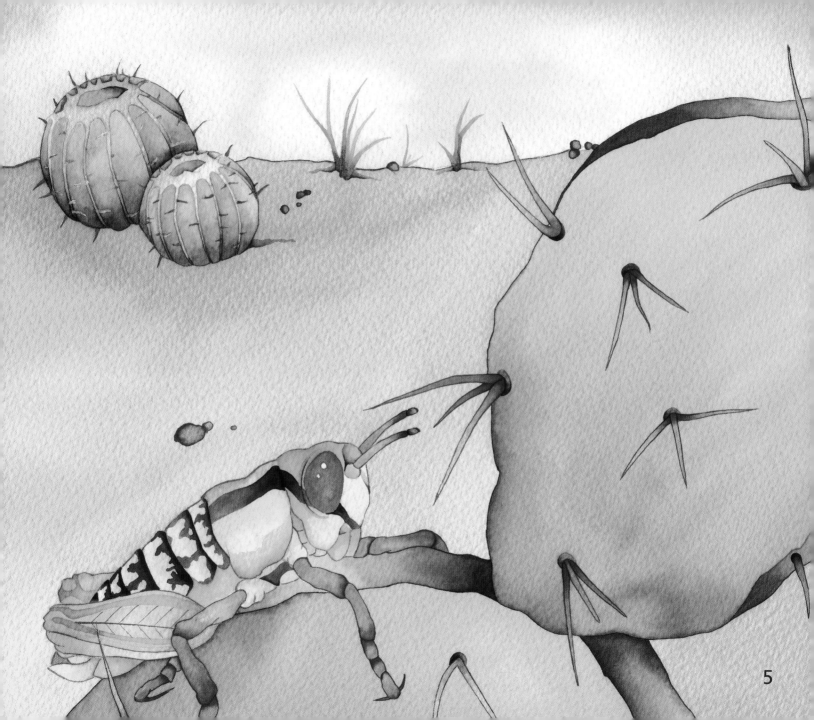

At first, the nymph's skin is soft, but the skin soon hardens. It becomes tough, like fingernails. The new, hard covering is the grasshopper's skeleton. It protects the insect's body like a suit of armor.

The grasshopper's body is growing, but its skeleton is not. After a few days, the skeleton breaks open. Slowly, the grasshopper crawls out. This is called molting.

The grasshopper's new, bigger skin is soft, but it will harden. A few days later, the new skeleton will break open, and the grasshopper will molt again.

After molting several times, the grasshopper becomes an adult. Its wings are fully grown.

Grasshoppers do not breathe through their mouths. They breathe through tiny holes in their abdomens, or the back part of their bodies. These holes are called spiracles.

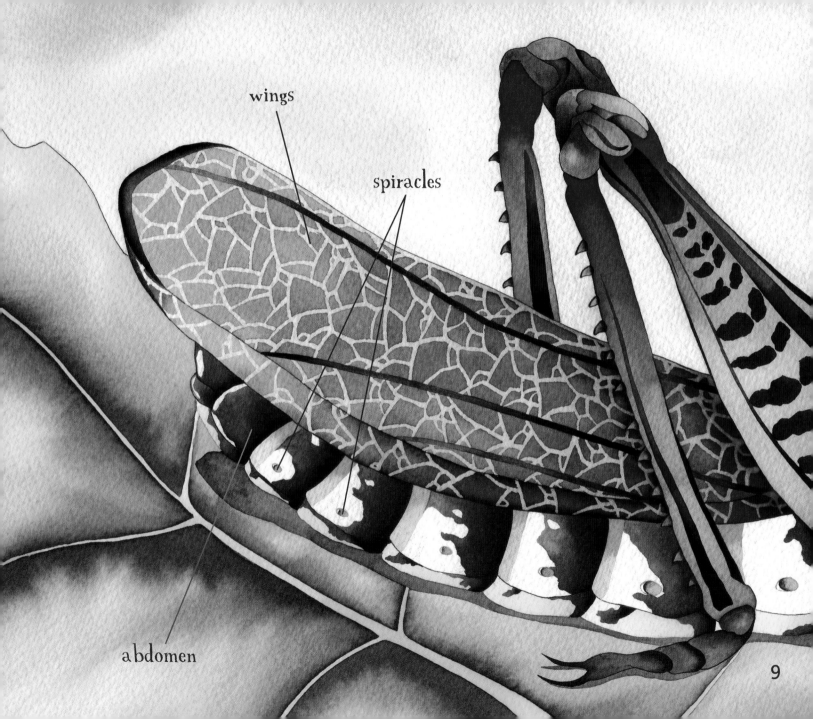

wings

spiracles

abdomen

9

Finding Food

Two grasshoppers are looking for grass to eat. One is a short-horned grasshopper. Its antennae are like thick, short sticks. The other is a long-horned grasshopper. Its antennae are as long as its body.

The grasshoppers wave their antennae. The antennae can smell, like a nose. They can touch, like fingers.

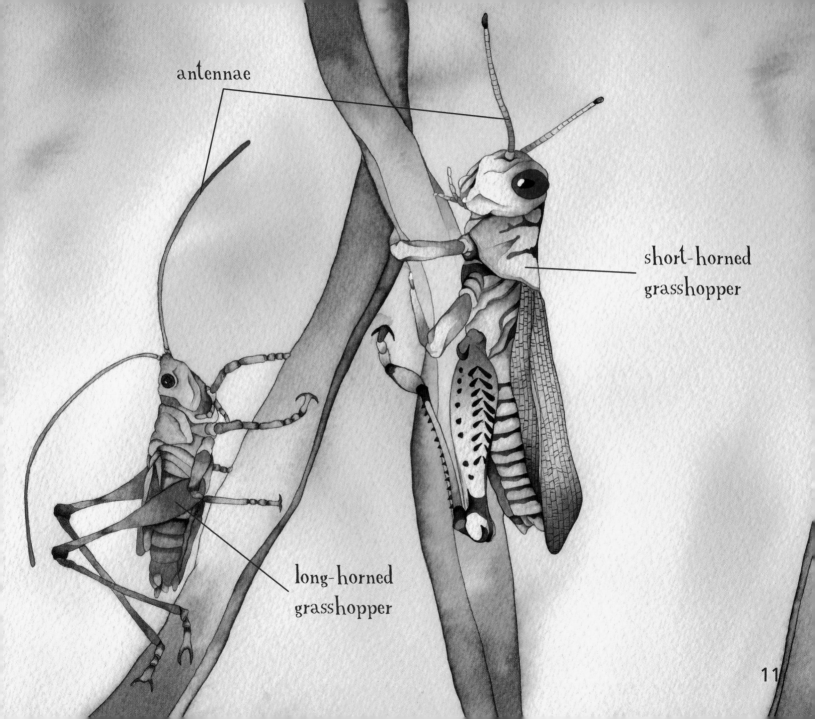

antennae

short-horned
grasshopper

long-horned
grasshopper

11

Most grasshoppers live and look for food alone. But one kind of grasshopper finds food another way. Grasshoppers called locusts swarm together. They look for food as a group. They fly together for many miles to find plants to eat.

Swarms of locusts can destroy entire crops.

Staying Safe

A grasshopper is always watching for predators. Its compound eyes help keep it safe. They are on the sides of its head. That lets the grasshopper see things coming from the side or from behind. Their special eyes can see moving things very well.

A human eye has one lens. It takes in a complete image all at once. A grasshopper's compound eye works differently. It has thousands of lenses. Each lens takes in a piece of the image, like a piece of a puzzle. This lets the grasshopper detect fast-moving things.

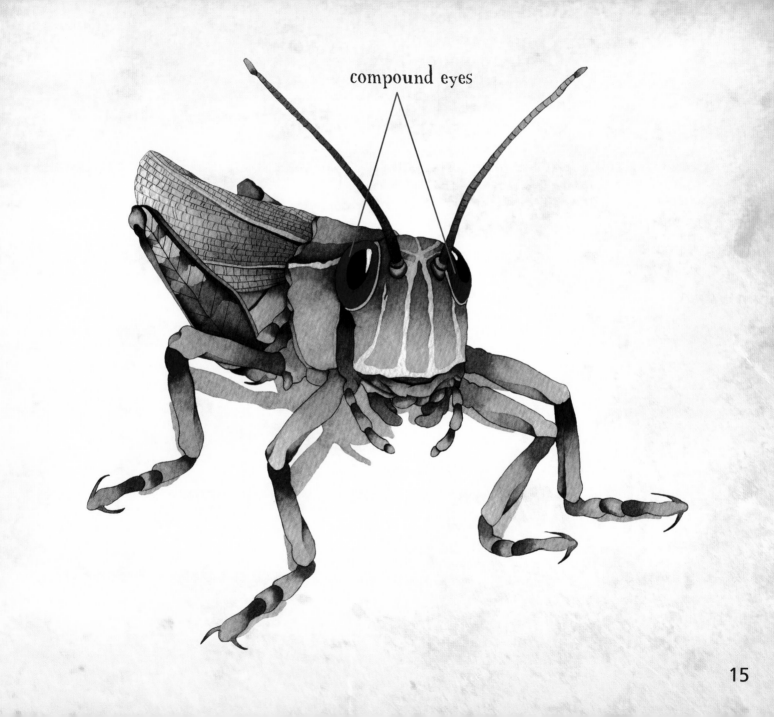

compound eyes

15

A grasshopper sees a flash of something coming closer.
A bird swoops down. It grabs the grasshopper in its claws.

The grasshopper spits out some brown liquid. That startles the
predator. The grasshopper has time to get away.

Hop, hop, hop. A grasshopper uses its strong back legs to jump far. Then it lifts its tough, leathery front wings. The thin, light wings underneath blur as they lift the grasshopper in flight.

Grasshoppers have six legs. They
use their first two pairs of legs to
walk and hold things.

Other grasshoppers are hiding. They go into the ground or deep into the grass. Some blend in with the leaves and rocks around them. Predators cannot see them.

More than 10,000 species of
grasshoppers live on Earth.

Musical Bugs

Summer is nearing its end. Outside, male grasshoppers are making beautiful music. The notes are to attract females.

Long-horned grasshoppers make music by rubbing their front wings together. Short-horned grasshoppers rub their legs against their wings. Each kind has its own special song.

22

Have you heard crickets chirp on a summer night? Crickets and grasshoppers are in the same bug family.

23

New Lives

Soon, female grasshoppers are laying eggs. They find a safe place in soil or on a plant.

The grasshoppers lay their eggs in a group called a pod. The female grasshopper squirts foam on the pod. The foam hardens, keeping the eggs safe and dry.

There is a chill in the air. Grasshoppers cannot live in cold weather. In cold climates, they die in winter. In spring, the eggs hatch. New grasshoppers begin their lives.

In warm climates, grasshoppers might live one to two years.

A Grasshopper's Body

A grasshopper's body has three main parts: the head, the thorax, and the abdomen. A grasshopper's skeleton is a hard, outer casing. It protects the grasshopper's soft body.

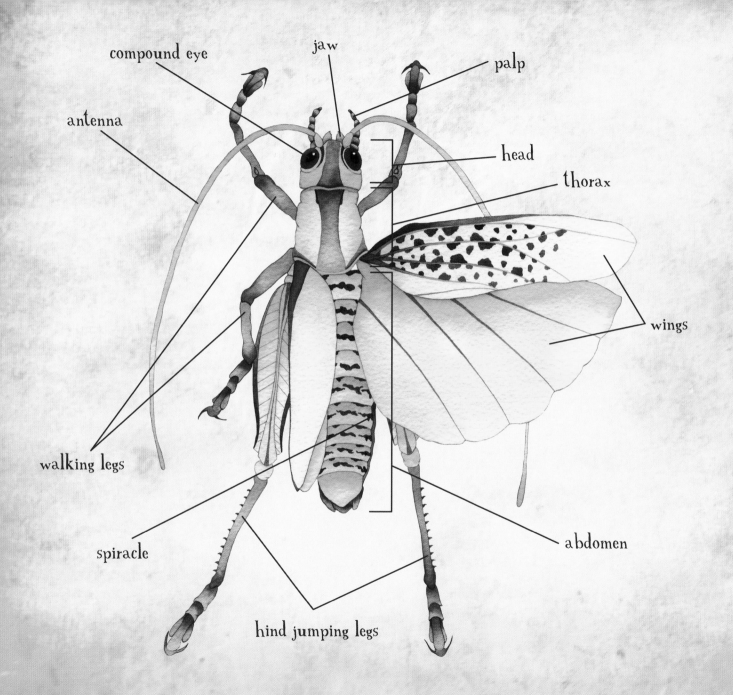

compound eye

jaw

palp

antenna

head

thorax

wings

walking legs

spiracle

abdomen

hind jumping legs

29

A Closer Look

Compare Short-horned and Long-horned Grasshoppers

What you will need:

- picture of a short-horned grasshopper
- picture of a long-horned grasshopper
- paper
- pencil

Look at pictures of a short-horned and a long-horned grasshopper. Divide the paper into thirds: a top, a middle, and a bottom.

At the top of the page, compare how the grasshoppers are the same. Below that, write how they are different. Use the bottom of the page to list the ways the grasshopper's features may be useful.

Here is an example to get you started:

How they are the same
Three main body parts
Outside skeleton

How they are different
Long-horned grasshopper has longer antennae

Helpful features
Tough outer wings protect thin flying wings

Grasshopper Facts

- When a grasshopper molts, it swallows a lot of air. The air puffs up the body. Then the outside skeleton breaks open.
- Grasshoppers are super jumpers. Some can jump **20** times their body length. That would be like a child jumping about the length of two school buses!

Glossary

abdomen—the back part of an insect's body.

antenna (an-**TEH**-nuh)—one of the two long, thin body parts that sticks out from an insect's head and is used to feel and smell.

compound eye—an eye made up of thousands of lenses, with each one taking in a piece of an image.

molt—to break out of a layer of skin so that new, bigger skin can grow.

nymph (**NIMF**)—a young grasshopper.

pod—a group of grasshopper eggs.

swarm—a large group of insects. To swarm also means to gather into a large group.

thorax—the middle part of an insect's body.

On the Web

To learn more about grasshoppers, visit ABDO Group online at **www.abdopublishing.com**. Web sites about grasshoppers are featured on our Book Links page. These links are routinely monitored and updated to provide the most current information available.

Index